A Life's Journey
(In Poetry)

JOSÉ SOARES

Printed by PublishingPush Ltd

Contents

ACKNOWLEDGMENTS

Throughout all these years of writing poetry I've been blessed by the people I've met and to one way or another they have pushed and inspired me to write.

Firstly, I like to thank my daughters for their support and inspiration with their poetry and philosophy book gifts. They are the reason that my world is filled with joy and happiness. Eleanor and Madalena love you lots.

I would like especially to give thanks to my nephew Angelo Encarnação for his contribution with his drawings for the book as well as his time on video calls from Paris and Lake Como in Italy.

Lastly, I would like to thank all my friends and followers on Facebook for their words of encouragement and support. A special thanks to Patrick Christy for being a friend and vivid reader, always pleasant with a positive outlook. His extraordinary charity work for Mobility Worldwide and his friends are an example of human light and compassion. Bless you all.

Joe Soares

BODY MISSED
BY JOE

Today like another day
A hard time at work
The smell of shit
And mountainous
Hardship
Like a showered world
Betrayed by money
Paper notes instead
But one's heart
Looks deeper
Pages unwritten
Books at play
For the next visitor
Tremendous amount
And other checks
Ink of library stories
Unspoken by tomorrow
All at sea wrecks
Things of a working life
But her beauty
Suave still
The wish that will
Walks one's drive
often the feeling
And long periods
One holds one breath
As a body moves
Quietly holding
My heart till death

A FLIGHT OF HOPE
BY JOE

At the beginning
of the Stars
The cosmic dust
Atomic database
The evolution
Awareness bringing
Consciousness
For some times afar
A flight that you must
An universe maze
Large and broad
Far as your imagination
Like a dance in Heaven
Not yet dreamed and told
But one's mind creation
A dreamlike glow
Not yet given
But a hopefully
Flightpath to grow

A FLOATING SOUL
BY JOE

Have you tasted the winds
Of everything
The love that is gone
Hiding invisible
Have you seen the winds
That is blowing
Intensively
One's deepest secret
Have you heard the winds
A song of a soul
Wondering
A root bud flowering
Higher than the skies
Have you lived the winds
Perched like a little bird
Asking to fly
As the arch of sunny light
And the night
Questioning for replies
Have you felt the winds
Of one's destination
The other side of life.

A FLOWER IN THE MIST
BY JOE

The shinning rays above cried your existence
Of yesterdays and tomorrow
Warming the mist of the forest
Creating a rainbow of sorrow
The same light of love

Through the density of all
Trees and arboreal madness
I saw you sitting down below
Arms crossing your chest
Like saying...where shall I go?

Minutes passed like hours pounding
A deer stared...paused, yet a rabbit ran fast .
A leaf smiled ... water -rain dropped
Awaking a long distant past...

A HUMAN WEB
BY JOE

One's universal living
So much to learn
Reservoir of emotions
A process of being
A space you can't run
Unknowing directions
But Earth knowledge
Kingdom of life knows
Beforehand
Things you can't understand
One's essences obscuring paths
Conditions of love
Thus reminiscences
Life and everything
As the pleasant breezes
Gifts of the universe
The sunset before the Moonlight
The smell of wooden
Forested trees
Free things of might
Beautiful as your soul
The mindful
True to living right.

A MAN OF WISDOM
BY JOE

I've lived before I was
I was a child
I knew the present
Unknowing all because
I had a dreamlike
Of a kind
Never knew who I was
wondering and exploring
The humankind
The good ones and bad
Some making you sad
Careless and ignoring
What's going in one's mind
A travelling soul
Searching for wisdom
Of a paradise Kingdom
Lost on this Earth
wishing we are all
Together as One
Creating uplifted love
Kindness from a birth
The lighthouse
Teaching you the light
Of one's parent's house
To know what's right.

A MYSTERIOUS LIFE
BY JOE

A world of questions
The exploring mind
One's quietly mentions
Of a man's intentions
A true wish and kind
The meaning of life
Wishing upon a purpose
A garden without a rose
The vastness land
Things to understand
Climbing upon dreams
Yet nothing is at it seems
A book of darkness
Read by living light
A courage of madness
Forcing greater high
Complex as one's soul
And others spiritual glow.

A NEW OPEN LIGHT
BY JOE

Where no sun shining
Trees of woodland hiding
Rays of sunshine
Welcoming the bright
Lights of wonder
A wishing star
The flow of wind and rain
Or a dried fruit in a deserted land
Hand in hand
A beautiful life
Wishing no pain
The elements of being
Stories untold
Of this world
People's imaginative
Poisoning true
Thinking of the mind
As me and you

A NIGHT WISH
BY JOE

This minutes
This hours
Seconds from the sky
A travelling light
Wishing you
By my side
The missing touch
And the kissing
Harbouring
Our love
An ocean's calmness
A magical time
Precious
As the night
Warm breeze
An overwhelming
Passion
A tide swelling
Inside
Floating around
And love hurts
Like songs
Of despair
A longing
A wish of the
Night.

A SPIRITUAL EMBRACE
BY JOE

Light years of voyages
Throughout all universe
Your mother Earth ages
As love seems to disperse

The searching of love
Humanity still dividing
What lies up above
As they hopefully finding

There is always light
Breathing in us inside
Eager hearts alight
That mutual coincide

There will be stars storms
Absorbing interstellar dust
Many blasting wormholes
Living on this Earth you must

A SUN HORIZON
BY JOE

While you sleep
Or awake
Night or day
Beneath
Or underneath
Lies one's soul
Looking for light
Quietly abandoned
To meditate
Of a tranquil dream
Love wishing
Uncertain sun rays
Thus far away
As the moon
And other stars
But the Sun
Warms the grass land
Like your yearning
Your search destiny
To find peace
As the clouds above
Slowly moving
One's unravelling path.

A TRACK UNKNOWN
BY JOE

In life you travel
With ups and downs
A world of marvel
Within us crowds

The searching of happiness
The pain learned
And all the distress
Something to be earned

A present living mystery
Of all earthlings souls
Unknowing what future be
As a living path unfolds

The road is mountainous
Of hard terrain and water
Or you are spontaneous
As Earth deceivingly torture

The deeper your voyage
Lies strength within
Wisdom and courage
Forges a man from a teen.

A TRAVELLING ENERGY
BY JOE

As love poetry goes
Written by the famous
And the infamous
A heart no one knows

But the affection by you
Traveling in my thoughts
As daily my soul must do
Aches like one's heart knots

Sweet as a smiling flower
On the fields yearning
A love for to adore her
Like a sunny day coming

A voyage filled with dreams
A contentment of wonder
like the flowing of streams
And skies without thunder

Like rain drops on flowers
Shining throughout
You shine highest powers
Of kindness many to count

Fruitfulness of an adventure
By a deeply beating heart
Where love is warm tender
One's embrace must start.

A WALK OF LIFE
BY JOE

There is many walks
Many paths you can take
But a grandad will make
That you follow his talks

He will hold your hand
Teaching love and wisdom
Things you can't understand
A future that is coming

He knows what may follows
A self-experience of living
To be old will be all of us
But a time lessons giving

He lived walking the walks
A life beforehand
Having sameness talks
With someone's hand.

A WARRIOR'S BEAUTY
BY JOE

She travelled the pain
A walker of paths unknown
She has felt
You know
Mountains of rain
A life
The days learning
Or a cry
Clearing sorrows
And asking why
This heart burning
A fire
Of ashes bygone
Far they seem
Like a dreamed
Love desire
Forever gone
Yet she's waiting
For a fighter
A lover
A man of her dreams.

A WIND'S WHISPER
BY JOE

It grew stronger
As she walked
By the sea shore
A starting breeze
That no longer
Caresses her face
Things she dreamed
Blowing away
And the clouds
Turning the blue skies
Mysterious and dark
And the Sun slowly
Without fire faraway
Weak weeping cries
Like the sombre dunes
Move by the silenced
And deadly winds
Echoing across
The thundering waves
Devouring pure white sands
A lifetime resemblance
Of luscious scents of love
Silky and soft
A gaze at the past
Fields of rose petals
Wishing them back
Flown out your hands.

ALL THIS LIFE
BY JOE

Till the end of time regardless
How beautiful is one's birth
Breathing all this mother Earth
And all above you
The Stars the Moon and the Sun
One's evidence of life you the daughter and son
A free paradise for you given
And all other species
For love living
Yet the Apple and the Snake
Poisoning what was at stake
Buddha will say what a mistake
With his benevolent smiling face
Sinful ungrateful human Race
Lost in a world without
Compassion
A living life without any
Reaction
Closed hearts of blindness
That one day you grow old
And cry for help yet helpless
How our physical body
Changes
But rejoicing love

EXPLORING ONE'S SOUL
BY JOE

Step by step a walk
A walking
The unknown voyage
The space between
Margins within thinking
The pace of one's mind
A rushing surviving
Emotional being
Human searching
Of a sweet paradise
Lost in disguise
Betraying path
A living bath
Of wrongdoing
Timeless on going
Showered by pain
And a savoury daily rain
Blessed by universal love
Things of life and soul.

FACES OF SPACES
BY JOE

Look around you
Feel the breeze
The unknown sky
That moment in time
Only you where you freeze
The world seems calm
Unlike faces imitations
Amongst living on this Earth
The love for people
This planet creations
Made of clay and dirt
A gift of happiness and pain
Shadows and light
A pour of storming rain
And winds turning bright.

HOLDING ON
BY JOE

With my bare hands
I catch your pain
Cos I'm not just a writer
I feel and understands
I'm an inside fighter
I catch a pouring rain
A nothingness
Like ocean's winds
Comforting a storm
Yet powerless
Feelings that swings
The love for you
The pain upon history
Close to one's heart
Dreamlike new
Or the end of story.

HUMAN DREAMS
BY JOE

From birth we dream
We dream a dream
Dreams come and go
A magical place
Beautiful land space
The traveling of minds
Dreaming all kinds
A universe unknown
Of Angels
Spiritual of visions
Guardians
Of heartlands
And streams of peace
Shadows of fear
A dreamy garden
Quietly disappear
The unknown love
Turning and turning
Pillow to pillow
The awakening from above
A sleepless land
Of glowing night stars
Day dreamers dream
Of happiness and sadness
Like a life of a dying rose.

I AM SOUL DANCER
BY JOE

I wrote about life extreme
I write about a river stream
Heading to a place unknown
I write about anything thrown

My mind is a world carousel
Some things I even can't spell
I talk languages vocal sound
But in silence I fly around

I have a dancing mind
I flow living of anything kind
One's universal souls spheres
This moment that disappears

I've many moon and sun dances
Mountains and ocean's circumstances
I write about anything
I dance joyfully as I think.

I WANT TO KNOW
BY JOE

Where the Stars come from
And dreaming about
The celestial love
Thoughts on my own
Things hard to believe
Like Earth going around
Between Heaven and hell
Angels and dark forces
A fight by morning and eve
A living spinning carrousel
A quest without destination
Like wild runaway horses
A mysterious creation
Like souls wanted the truth
And the meaning of life
Wishing upon a star
Like me and all of you
Free of a madness world
Hold the full moon
Be what you think and are
Summers and winters
Or morning and afternoon
Just another time note.

JUST DREAMING
BY JOE

A pathway
Same as a nightly
Sleeping
A gateway
Doors of dreaming
Opening slightly
A field view
Of waterfalls
Eyelashes of wonder
As painter drew
Things out of souls
That we all conquer
Dormant
In silence
An ocean's flows
She lives within me
Like seagulls flying
A dream
That she's arriving
To be with
By my side.

JUST THINKING
BY JOE

By the sea shore
I wasn't so sure
The love that I adore
Wherever the cure
maybe winds of whispers
Calming one's longing
And a heart full of tears
Hopelessly hanging
Perhaps for the love lost
Staring at the moment
Or counting the cost
Of living a real torment
Yet life's experience
Happy for a time
Sadness an existence
Maybe yours or mine
The grey turned to Sun
Winter to summer
A light brightening run
And waves forgotten drama.

LIFE...LOVE AND PARADISE
BY JOE

We all pray everyday
Not in a church
Or in a monastery
But day by day you search
Your life mystery
Quite forgotten in your soul
Born to love
Like Springfield's aromas
Flown by butterflies
Or by wings of a dove
The silent of inner dramas
Murmurs of cries
Drifting thoughts
Wishing life clears
Simply as morning sun
But those tight knots
Of Heaven and hell tears
Showers of an endless rain
Corridors of mountainous rivers
Like songs of despair
A restlessness of feelings
One seems not to care
Of the pain meanings
But a river sings along
Trusting the rocks for melodies
Savouring the water's stream
Making your voyage strong
And the wish your dream
Across your own stories.

MY LIFE... MY WORLD
BY JOE

I'm a Warrior
And nature my mother
I'm a survivor
Like no other
I'm the Eagle's flight
And the wolf's roar
All powerful fight
destined to soar
I'm waves free
Like the winding oceans
Kissing ashore thee
Crying deep emotions
I'm strength upon the skies
As my walk by the river
Letting my solitude cries
Running timeless deeper
I'm the peaceful guardian
Guided by the Great Spirit
Where peace is uniquely one
Upon a mountain summit.

MYSTERIOUS IS LIGHT
BY JOE

Think of the universe
Awake your dormant mind
Walk away out of chaos
See the secrets of life
Invoke spiritual love
Run away from guilt
Dance above the sky
As a smiling white dove
Thoughts of the best kind
Rejuvenate your soul
Transform and tilt
Who cares if you cry
Same as flames of a fire
Dancing away momentum
Warming your distance mind
Conquer your love within
Your emotional desire
And the luminosity stardom.

ONE MORE HOUR
BY JOE

I will sleep one more hour
Before the sun rises
I will dream
My hopes
My universe
Stars away far
And the light
Of the Moon
Gathering of galaxies
Disperse thousands
Of miles away
Thoughts
Traveling
Towards a mountainous
Sea
In a boat of love
Just one more hour
Before the sun rises
I dream
A lifetime dream
To be with you
Together where
The sunsets
And the hoping
Breeze
Gathers our souls

THE AUTUMN NIGHT
BY JOE

The fall of the winter
A moonlight whisper
Secrets of an inspire place
As you smile and hear
A softening lift of light
Leafs helplessly falling
Dancing away in tenderness
Coloured by winds of time
Yesterday's blooming life
Shadows of being regardless
Whose brunches you belong
As the sunlight makes you strong
Bright as a morning sky
Then you ask darkness why
Why we live yet to die
As the daylight and night
A sun and moon romance
Watching raindrops of Autumn
Holding in togetherness hands
Smiling that life never ends.

THE BOOK OF WISDOM
BY JOE

In life you follow the path
The road unknown
The pain
A breath of truth
A wreck beneath
Stolen by webs of time
Floods sucking mind
Nothing and everything
A teaching of life
Stealers of dreams
A glowing spark
A play of entertainment
Triumphs of life's choices
A perceived reality
Of light and dark
The sentiment of emotions
A conquer of love
Heights enduringly
A passion promised
The abundance
Soaring higher
And higher
A promise awaiting
A prayer

THE FLIGHT OF LIGHT
BY JOE

The simplest riding
The light within
The love far gone
The wishing
The meaning
The precious time
The traveling
The unknown
The highest stone
The power of a soul
The climbing
The purpose of it all
The distress
The happiness
The moment
The searching
The freedom
The universe
The walk in space
The reason
The bursting
The flight
The human race.

THE FLYING WIND
BY JOE

Imagine the waves
From distant afar
Cries of a deserted land
And only
The lonely sand
Flying dunes of love
And yesterday's rages
Brushing the past
Away...
Away yet slowly
Passing
Transformed in time
Letting go
Where breezes flow
And changes become
On a westerly wind
Systematic
Every day as my love
For you
And you never will go
Cos your beauty
Dramatic
Must stay
And you know
The winds will change
But I will never go away.

THE LAMP OF WISHING
BY JOE

Of a life unlived
Earth's a stage
A gaze
Shadows of the night
Dreams that you believed
A fireplace conversation
A deep chant
Between you
And dancing flames
A wish a want
Imagination
Love has gone
Life goes on forever
Forgotten blames
The power of a soul
And the pain
Ever experienced
Which I know
Pierced by dropping rain
Valleys separated
And a solitaire moon
Tender as passion
A voice and whispers
Starlit night glowing
As the hushed morning
A breeze softness
Awaking a genius
Of dormant thousand years.

THE LIES OF HUMANS
BY JOE

We always wonder
The truth of friendships
Why the skies thunder
And the oceans ships
Quit on sailing
Why believing in winds
That inner pain brings
The longing of prevailing
Porky porky pies
Those little lies
The trustworthy
Gone by waves
Of discovery
A believe that takes
You and me
The trust dying
Lost at sea
Wrecks of surviving
At a shore arriving
As you see.

THE NATURE OF WRITING
BY JOE

And then there is you
A humanist
Therefore you exist
Within nothingness
But thoughts beneath
Of existential wilderness
The wisdom of thought
A trembling scribbling pen
A spirited soul got caught
By in a silence imagination then
Then... all happens
Thereafter is breeding life
Like seasoned coming hours
Of winds of Autumn scribe
The winter stormy powers
And the springtime flowers
A summer sunlight
A world of beautiful delight
Bursts of a mind and anything

THE ORIGINS OF LOVE
BY JOE

A spectrum of light
A nuclear fusion
A primordial universe
Quartz and neon
Exploding waves bright
Atmospheric noise collision
Creation of mighty bond
Filled by oxygen abundance
Moving galaxies disperse
Thousands of miles a second
Forging elements eternal
And the growing infinity
Springing into existence
The antimatter debris
Particles from deep afar
A Cosmos persistence
Like beings on Earth radar

THE SPARK
BY JOE

Up the sky I've looked
Behind stimmy window's
Mirror
But nothing just me
A face of reflection
Tears running down
As the outside rain
Because all these years
Walked a road unknown
Like tonight's cold
A human travelling
One's passing ground
Experienced tales
Voices made of clouds
Untrue by the harvest
Of a wet September
Like the rising Moon
Shining biggest
Dancers of invisible songs
And field workers
Soul giving all
An applause silenced
The comets higher
Higher light.

THE WAITING
BY JOE

Looking into dead stones
Years like the moonlighting
And winds of you arriving
Like warming musical tones

A solitude of a soul lonely
Wishing the love of you
A rain of time drops slowly
Of an empty space too

Why my throne is so cold
When my Kingdom is vast
Life appears to be so old
Till have found you at last

The pain that I endured
Of a wet freezing path
Until you became the cure
Giving me warm-hearted bath

The last encounter of magic
Staying like auras of infinity
Forever away from tragic
Becoming you and me.

THIS EARTH * THIS LOVE
BY JOE

I see adventures coming
Like a splashing
Of tender pleasure
Or whatever
A love that you always seek
A tree to hug and meet
Close to mine
A sweet flower
Born in the wild
Raised by mountains high
A bliss of marvel
Discovered by a traveller
An explorer of love
A multitude of reasons
Like an eluded dream
Paved by all seasons
Whereby a kiss of nature
Nourishing a water stream
Consumed by Earth's fire
The sweet explosion
And passion deep
Searching desire.

TO BE FREE
BY JOE

Come with me
Where a dark place
Is awaiting
Come do come
And look in darkness
Feel what I feel
Open your eyes
And what you see
Corridors like a maze
Yet betraying
What will become
As the unknowing skies
And this present Inverness
Do not hush and run
Experience a snowfall
Cooling your passage
Await for the light
Lightening your pathway
Look for the coming Sun
Arising for me and all
No matter one's age
Or race black and white
Because it's Heaven's way.

A CONTENTMENT OF WONDER
BY JOE

This is our precious Earth
A soul pleasing
That colours one's spirit
The distant moonlight
Crying and pleading
Turning oceans full of tears
Of hurt
Just imagine sitting
Or in this shores lying
Your sinful body
Enjoying the light of the night
Reminiscing
Thinking of love
Or peace for the world
Breathing a nightly freshness
Aromas of the sea blue
The quietness of the mind
The rights and wrongs of living
One's awareness
A peaceful time of compassion
For your steps on the clear sand
You will never understand
But your worldliness.

WHEN A MAN'S BROKEN
BY JOE

We build castles
Engulfing structure
They say man's nature
And living hassles
They say the biggest liar
A world of gossip
While a drink you sip
Senses one's acquire
Listen to the wind's life
As steep as it seems
Climb your voyage
Runaway full of courage
As a mountain dreams
Wishing the snow go
And the streams
Rugged by the hills
One heart that feels
Forever years ago
The love of a woman
Cold as mountains high
Communication goes by
Strangely a lovely man
A sweetheart....
Just saying darling
Not a broken heart

WHY RUNAWAY
BY JOE

A sea of love destroyed
Upon a sailing moon
And waves bygone
Like a showered cyclone
Raves almost forgone
But one's soul annoyed
By this time of darkness
Beneath a moonlight
Awaiting a sunlight
Of a morning bright
Wishing rich brightness
Like a smile of goodbye
A running sea of dreams
Afar from river streams
A living life it seems
Of this Earth... why

WHY THE UNIVERSE
BY JOE

Everything
The sky above
The unknown mystery
A love of this deep Earth
The One that is gone
By wings of desire
A wave of this day
Flown by disarray
One's moment hurt
To be forgotten
Hidden from ocean's salts
And dunes opened to life
Sands of hurtful true
A never ending crying
Seas born of a wind
Paradise mare results
Till a black hole
The unknown blow
A shining will bring
Tell you how deep
Is your love

AN ANGEL PAIN
BY JOE

At times you not loved enough
You feel filters of pain
Things of inside
Thoughts and dreams
Burning one's heart out
Voices never been heard
A true lovely wish
Between a world of magic
Abandoned and absurd
Being poor or ever rich
Everything of this Earth
Lives and dies
Wonderfully tragic
The world we live in
Pain upon rivers of pain
Tears running for years
One's soul lives between
This life and an angel tears
The highest help of your cries.

THE WAVES OF LIFE
BY JOE

The Sun brightness
Waves sparkling dancing beyond
One's darkness
A deepest blue sea
Sinking one's soul
In loneliness
A cry of lashing water
A silence ultimately be
Washed upon ashore
Sands returning again
Braking uncertain waves
A tide wishing land
Diving to treasures lost
A dancing of the braves
Of the sky and sea
Warriors of light
Beneath and above

THE RED IN YOUR BLOOD
BY JOE

Like a voyage of time
Wishing you near
But far
My dear you are
The kisses missed
Flavours of lips
Never known
Like a sunset
Untouchable trips
Away out of an horizon
Thus far we never met
Moving in other space
Rainbows of mystical colours
A longing red rose
Searching a kind of race
Of a garden light
As love lovingly arose.

THE HAND OF LIGHT
(A gift from Patrick Christy)

Understanding one's kindness is living
Is doing with real compassion
The gifted
Lessons directed
By thunderstorms
The lifetime of wisdom
The calling
The light unreal
But inside
The freedom
One's whispering times
Envisioned by human
Hurt
The needed
As the sun will bring the sunshine
Few realise
The hurting humankind
Maybe the morning will bring
Back the light
Open as the hands
Of daylight Spring.

SCATTERED LOVE DUST
BY JOE

As time old passes by
I look for you at night
I search amongst all stars in the sky

Passing memories
Passing times
But the wind`s crying
It seems for centuries

A blast from the past
Spreading our love forever
A flash in a pan
Flying through all the universe dust

Sometimes I do think of you
I wonder if you ever think of me
I have you in my heart till the end of time
As the moon cannot live without the sun
You belong to me you are mine

Sometimes I do think of you
I wonder if you ever think of me.

A SLEEPLESS NIGHT
BY JOE

Whirling still my thoughts
And what nots
One wonders about life
It self
What I will do
To myself
I cannot sleep
Restlessness night
Turning deep
Crashing floors
Emptiness
Like open doors
Echoing
A state of madness
My soul disrupted
Tangled
By the thought of you
A dream of lustrous love
Golden crystallised
And the cosmic above
On this Earth paradise
Symphonies
Of anxieties
A painful passage
Taunting the night
But silence captures
One's destined voyage
A love not foreseen
Only imaged
Like an Angel keen
And save you
That life kicks you
On the chin

A blanket covers
Your skin
Like a dream.

A BOY'S LIFE
BY JOE

As far one's remember
The days of real fun
February or September
We played and run
We ran for living
Happy being there
Co.'s the believing
Was happiness everywhere
A voyage of a child
Without any baggage
Carrying a youthful wild
Love unknowing garbage
Thus waiting for true
Along within the present
That was and is you
One's own innocent
And loving moments
Of glorified childhood
Times without torments
But a walk in the wood.

A CARING LOVE
BY JOE

Those who are in love
As time is magic
Coming romancing above
Something unexperienced
A first need
Of kisses and hugs
A blissfully ride
A garden of extremes
Like a flower seed
Rooted by the sun side
And rain mountain's floods
The togetherness
Of ever season
Summer or Inverness
Yet colours of Spring
A life's greatest reason
And the love you will bring

A CHILDHOOD
BY JOE

Remembering
Those times
A pattern
Of destiny
As a friend
A song
Of a forest
When life's
Singing
Dancing birds
Soothing
Like yesterday's
Sun shine
A silly dance
Of life
Till you grow
Growing older
The closeness
Burned by distance
A sweetness
Of friendship
Years ago
The bloom
And gloom
Of a flower
The rise and fall
Like dropping tears
All this years .

A CULTURE PAIN
BY JOE

This Earth of ours
Only for a few hours
The love within us
Maybe seconds thus
This creation adrift
I must deeply admit
Going pear shaped
Destroyed and raped
By generations of hate
A collective us ache
Humanity crashes
Going to plunged ashes
Born to love...yet
Yet...man isn't correct
He hates the other side
A culture thing of blindness
Dormant subways
Surrounded by ignorance
As time goes it's ways
A believe of God
As the fear of death
Books of religious said
about humanity
A togetherness harmony
Contrary to loving
The upmost harnesses
Simple as living

A FLAMING LOVE
BY JOE

Sweet is the burning
Deep of heart's fire
Sleep of warmth

Light of loving
Bright as candles
Right there and near

Weep of dying love
Weak in deepest peace
Leap of a dreaming night

Sky of stirring breezes
High as the rising Sun
Flight of deepest touch

Spark beneath one's soul
Dark that no longer exists
Arch of sweet embrace

A GUARDIAN ANGEL
BY JOE

The hopping dreams
My usual flight
Growing waves of displeasure
The strangling mind
A hole that profound
Eating out my flesh
All life that seems
Nothing going right
Searching one's hidden treasure
A resistant man's kind
Soaring for a love around
Finding one's conquest
Frowns of future
As a silenced wisp
And the ardent
Soul
Powerless feelings
Subdued by being unloved
But by an angel
Wish.

A LOVE JUST IN
BY JOE

Highlander to I am
To where I came from
Devoted to my Truelove
Just like oxygen
Coming from above
Above mountains high
The winds of passion
Life and love
Our beauty to share
Freely like the oceans
The abundant joy
From a sunny day
Coming to shore
The embrace
Of sandy beaches
And kiss the one
I adore
For us to explore
Take a look of life stories
A book never told
Unique memories
A journey of life
A pleasant satisfaction
Of this generous world
A loving journey
To love her .

A LOVE WANTED
BY JOE

Our spirituality
So complex
One's infinitum
Entwining
Mixing
A cocktail
Souls travelling
An eternity
Hearts of love
By life betrayed
A song of wonderland
Breaths of Moonlight
Newfound nights
Leaps of dreams
One's deep sensitivity
Exalted silences
Sleepless darkness
Rhythms of inner voices
Timeless thoughts
Saturating time hours
Impulses of destiny
Expectations
Senses of illusions
Like the rising light
Carrying warmth
Seduction of lust
Wrapped by comfort
Of one's completeness
Feeling alone yet empty

A MYSTICAL LOVE
BY JOE

O mind of mine
Distracted
By a simple wish
A stillness
A glowing light
Peaks of a mountain
Mystic
Flowing cloudy streams
Illuminating
The field below
Where flowers
Are an illusion
Sweetness
The road to go
A runway lover
Swimming a river
And the rocks
Stones in water
Sharpness of a soul
A tumbling West
Or East
Like the Moon
Over the valley
And the mountain range
Shutter your dreams
From the North
The darker of winds
Blowing into Sea
And nothingness
But thoughts
Became
Waves of loving you.

A SHOWER AFTER
BY JOE

The simplest touch of your hand
That always make me wiggle
The wet of love no end
Between us we niggle

A kiss softness taste
Like a forever river flow
Sweet...soft...and slow
Timing one's haste

Skin to skin we feel
The sweetest movement
Up and down a lovely hill
A body to put one's dormant

Yet I can listen to your silence
The pain you cannot hold
Being one's trouble no sense
Amidst the warmth and cold

A beautiful lovely spirit soul
A voyager of life deep desire
As crystallised waterfall
Awaiting to rock and roll.

A WHITE FEATHER'S EYE
BY JOE

It fell on my kitchen floor
Hence the picture
A message
Of spirit
Why does happen for
I'm afraid I won't understand
Is it for faith or destiny
For darkness or light
Or love coming to an end
Maybe I'm blessed
And let love to grow
Like warming rays
Bright ling if you are stressed
There is no existing sound
Words or winds within
A captured moment
For a poem going around
It seems to look at you
At an unbelievable world
Like a dove's travelled eyes
And all things you do.

A WOMAN'S BEAUTY
BY JOE

Thinking of romancing
Things of loving
Our inner voices
A land of dreaming
Whispering choices
Who loves me
A soul pleasing
Or us forever
Drowned in the sea
Her body of night pleasure
One's devotion
And intensity
like embraces of treasure
There inside I want her
Dreams that one's have
Clear and vivid
Imagination
Thoughts
you can't control floods of kissing
Breathless deeply
And what nots
About things you can't have
But shared memories
Because her beauty
I still have and keep
For my moments and histories.

AND THERE SHE IS
BY JOE

Between two mountains
Forgotten world
A lost paradise
I've been long told
There lives a glowing pearl
A radiant smile
Light that I become to feel
Or the wind's whisper
A thunder's calling
A shout of a tremor
Alive and dreaming
A precious being
Filled by fortunes
Blessed by nature
A reason beyond time
A glimpse
A love story breath
Kissing upon air
Drifting since
The ocean's return
And believing
That her kind of eyes
Are smiling
As the winter's Sun.

BECASE OF YOU
BY JOE

The memories
Of you
Timeless hours
The lips
Forever kissed
Of a night
The silent dance
Under the rain
The embrace
Missed
A dreamy garden
Full of pleasure
Histories
A fruit of love
Fantasies of winter
A seasonal desire
The light of dawn
Freshly blossoms
A flower
Raised by the sun
Pulsing rhythms
Of a rotating Earth
You afar tonight
The wish
Of being with you.

COLD AS FIRE
BY JOE

In physics cold burns
In life warm returns
The love going by
The one that you cry

Seasons of time caged
Seasons of winter enraged
Inside a heat glows
Inside a fire blows

A misty morning is cold
A passion to be unfold
An embrace of lovers
An embrace under covers

As the mountain winds
As the rivers colds brings
The crisp of a lovable breeze
The fire that within freeze.

COLOURS OF THE SKY
BY JOE

Ask me why
How beautiful is the sky
Rains and winds
Lighting above brings
One's soul high
Smiling forever by
As the beauty of Earth sings
Of love and compassion
Glowing happiness
A planet breathless of passion
A summer's heat
Or a winter's freeze
Gardens of peaceful glow
Like fields of barley and wheat
Feeding a coming snow
Radiant illumination
Of a rainbow
Soul deep imagination
Streams of living
Perspective light beams
Of the sun and moonlight dreams.

FOR YOU WITH PASSION
BY JOE

Deep within my breath
And the darkness of the night
The voices whispering
Before one's death
Our passion away
Wet with passionate fire
Continuous to stay
A time overwhelming
Touches and kisses
Times of desire
Crazy feelings
A body heat
One's heart beat
Real time meanings
Words are not never enough
But the feeling for you
Everyday grows
Stronger and stronger
Love and the kind stuff
That no one knows
But I deeply do.

HANDS OF WISDOM
BY JOE

In your hands is your
Traveling soul
Your hard work
Joyous memories
And forever
Remaining
The experience
A school of ages
To understand
One's essences
Obscuring paths
And the true awaiting
A return
A suffering world
Turning life pages
do not surrender
Be joyful
Gather a storm
Embrace the winds
Wherever the cold
Move
Feel the warmth
Of a coming dawn
A sunlight
That will bring
A childhood smile
Before you're old.

ICE COLD
BY JOE

I dream about anything
I'm awake I dream I think
Thinking just thinking
Dreamlike awaking
Awakens one`s desire
I walk along
Because I lied
To myself within fire
Chained by currents strong
Water's bridges of one's mind
A worldwide gazing
Of a love amorous
Time to time
Most times amazing
Yet the hidden lie
A frozen mysterious
Rosen within the sky
Crossing paths of love
Of snow country side
The warmth between us
Richer then a golden meadow springtime.

LIFE IN YOUR HANDS
BY JOE

The memories of yesterday
Alone walking
Doomed by living
Into to valleys day
The rains falling
Nothing yet given
But ash clouding winds
From a volcano afar
The trembling Earth
Pain deceiving
Stabbed yet no scar
A red light of a sky
Blowing up voices of colours
Something inside cry
The cries of light
Away from a wicked world
A highly compassionate power
Reach by the soul loving where ever the night
The day week month
Or one's happy beautiful hour.

LOVE IMPERFECT
BY JOE

Living behind nights
Gifts of words
Visions that go by
A make of minds
Our self's divine
Beings slumbering
By climbing a wish
Or a mountain high
A stream a river or a ocean
An emotional agony
A tempestuous flow
Darkened quickly
By his adieu
A shadow of tears
Upon her face
A Queen of fantastic realm
A book of the night
Voices of the secret
A flush of one's life
Like perpetual years
Us creators of calm
Delicate Angels
Against currents of debris
Struggling with pain
And fear of changes
But always been the horizon
The colourful wishing sky
There every minute
Very simply
A pulse of love.

MISSING YOU
BY JOE

The silenced room
A night without you
Emerging thoughts
My soul in dire knots
The talking outside
You by my side
Savouring the night
The voices of winds
And planes flying by
Forever our love brings
A barking loving dog
Chasing a fox jumps
Any time of dark or fog
Funny ferocious rumps
A tobacco smoked
Waves blown unspoked
The flowing magical
Of a time when you're
Close and personal
The way we know
Strong our feelings grow.

PAIN IS FIRE
BY JOE

Listen to life
And the whispering winds
Whistles of nature
One's innocence gone
By storms of existence
Culture human rules
And a suffering world
A world yet unknown
Mystical yet mysterious
Valleys of darkness
Mountains of light
The sacrifice
Armoured shields
Those tears alone
Being aware yet a prisoner
Blow after blow
Pretending inner voices
Hell and Heaven
Each and every day
Thoughts of peace and comfort
The love in our hearts
Misunderstood

PARADISE ON EARTH
BY JOE

The unknown living
Not in poems
Or the written word
But the happiest mind
Or sized by a sword
But by flower stems
And the garden of Heavens
Freshly blossoms
One's soul
The green of Spring
And the sunshine
The song of birds
and the stillness
Of voices of wood
A walk of spiritual
A passage with a smile
Jubilant in harness
The sun the sea waves
The moon and winds
Joyous living
One's smell of Earth

SHADES OF COSMOS GREY
BY JOE

Believing the heavens
The unknown universe
Engineering mind
The worth of humanity
Clueless of the proverbial
The miracle of an apple
And a snake of death
(Wtf. Me thinking)
A curse of pain
In the shadow
A captivating life
Written permission
By fortunes of time
The Cosmos debate
While you struggling
Awaiting for a super nova
Sentence to death
And die pure as love
Or of delighted compassion
And dearest beloved nature
Moments of enchanting Earth
The oneness we share
The cool breeze
Sensual aromas of a wind
Paradise sands
Land of spices
Meeting Heaven's gate.

TAVIRA BEAUTIFUL TOWN
BY JOE

As I was growing up
I've played of fields of yesterday
Na Atalia of bare feet football
Same story in Santa Luzia
A kid of coming 9 years old
Or 10 away far from today
A town of beauty
Transform by time
Yet it keeps her luz do dia
A light of this day
Breathing friendly openness
Welcoming strangers
Bathing in Tavira island
Savouring the warmth of sands
The sea summer horizons
And the best food imagined
My late father's fishing sea
My dear mum vegetable soups
Moments I cry and see
As I am writing by sorrowful hands

THE DAWN
BY JOE

One day I've departed
I fell into the abyss
Lost in the ocean's life
Tossed by winds unguarded
One's voyage
A step a fall a miss
Mistaken by sorrowful drive
A wreckage beyond help
Like a sinking dying ship
I was no captain baggage
Washed by unruly emotions
Drowning your spiritual soul
Into the horizons of nothing
Glazed by dreaming
Of a coming sunny day solutions
A tomorrow's swimming goal
Born to wishing surviving
Strength of human being
Strong as the sunlight
Rays of reason
As light embracing you.

THE FAREWELL
BY JOE

A day gone by
As the air is feeling fresher
And the green of smells
Comes a goodbye
The return of meadows sweet
Like dreaming winds
Descending from the sky
A place of solitude
Transformed peace
Because you know why
A love of pleasure
Enchanting moments
And learn how to fly
A beginning to be lived
Times cherished
And to soar above high
Life of encountered souls
Nomads of desired chemistry
As love becomes dry
A night kissed by the moon
Like a candle dancing flame
Put out by the morning cry
Tears of yesteryears
The light of today
Like a flying butterfly

THE GIVEN SUNLIGHT
BY JOE

Beyond the shadows of time
The human playfulness
This crowd divine Earth
Made of souls
Spirits of light
Born to live and die
Language of Gods
Travellers of the unknown
Like pain it's a lonesome cry
Wishing love and be loved
A soft life misguided
And beliefs
Created by untruths
Poisoned by dark shadows
Blocked unreasonable sky
Distantly your horizon goes
Lost in wilderness of time
Till a welcoming wind
Your heart heal
All sorrows as time still
And light discovers you.

THE LAST TOUCH
BY JOE

A falling rain cascading
Waters of happiness
Drops on you radiating
A smile nonetheless

A site of beauty to behold
Like the pouring rain drops
Kissing both hands like gold
The lovable love never stops

A yesterday's sunny day
Brightening your heart
But the rain came to play
Washing us distant apart

A luscious of times spent
A fever growing strong
Touching waters current
A course that went wrong

By day and by night
The unknown skies give
Opening a window bright
To smile again and forgive .

THE MAN
BY JOE

He is sometimes grumpy
Annoying
The slow descent
A rhythm of crescendos
A sway of pleasure
With mysterious eyes
Known existence
A persona prisoner
Of a muddled path of love
A commander
Yet powerless for loving
A Earth jewel
Following softly the winds
He loves to love
Enveloped in night dreams
Sacred to his own soul
Planning conquests far gone
But a tastefully life
Fluidity of loneliness
Echoing walls
Turned upside down
The power within
Of a man's world

THE ONE LOVE
BY JOE

The fruit of Eden
Given from Heaven
A God's wishing
A woman from above
A heartfelt of wonder
One's heart of thunder
The seasons beating
The breaths of pain arose
Your breath is my breath
Conquered by the seas
And higher mountains
Our butter and bread
Upon this earth
Slaves of a Kingdom of love
Strangers of running streams
Destined rivers
Oceans of gathering waves
Blown from moonrise winds
As cloudless dreams
Voices unheard
In one's silenced memory
Like a flying bird
Home returning
Joyfully.

THE REALLY TRUE LOVE
BY JOE

True love is from the heart
Not written or said words
Things from deep inside
A kiss softness taste
Caressing her hair all night
A fresh stream
A sweetheart dream
Tenderly forever bright
A woman's whispering
And holding her tight
A gift of the Heavens
As she lays her head
On one's chest
When nothing is said
But the loving rest
Yet the edge of temptation
Feebly as one's pleasure
A love seduction
And glows of imagination
But loving is the option.

THE SEAS OF LOVE
BY JOE

A morning sea breeze
After the gone moonlight
The love making
Like one's bursting
An exorbitant
Endless hours of tease
A timeless pleasure night
As the sun arising
Awakening
Your beautiful lips
Passionately kissed
A needed touch
As our souls smiling
The commitment of time
A change of living
Not to be missed.

THINKING OF YOU DEEPEST
BY DAD

With a heart of gold
Since she was born
A daughter to be called
MADALENA a fighter
Inspirational delight
Day or night
A caring beautiful soul
Full of life
My heart a breath
Until sleeping
My little girl angel
Emotions of agitation
Yet a sense of relief
By her courage
And stubbornness
Give me temper
And pride
To have her caring mind
Not forgetting
The largest pain
One's moment
Like a real torment
A Gemini's time
Only the moon bright
And the morning sun
Smiling triumph

YOU AND THE MOON
BY JOE

Tonight like any night
The arisen up high
A moonlight
Descending upon you
The past profoundly you knew
The rotating mind
Thinking of a kind
Thoughts going by
This glowing sky
Far aboveground
Higher than any sound
Beaming of brightness
Peace and kindness

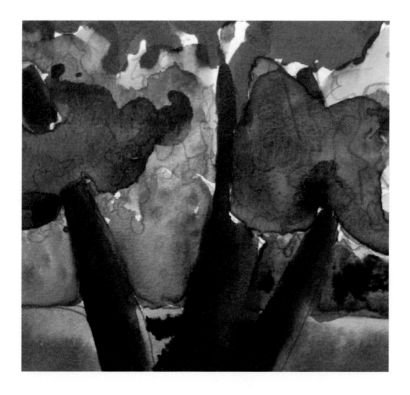

WISHING LOVE
BY JOE

The unknown and mystery
Magical shadows
Bright and dark
Deep within our sensitivity
Gleams of rainbows
Twinkling a spark
A wild wind dancing
Near to a loving soul
A shivering rising light
Inside romancing
A reminder recall
Of a biting winter night
A journey half crossed
Through a mountain river
And rushing down waterfalls
Around you are tossed
Bathed by life's endeavour
And secrets of night falls.

WHY A WOMAN
BY JOE

Why a woman touches my heart
With your body so young
It sets my soul on fire
Aflame by a fragrance of desire
Why a woman is like you
More beautiful than any flower
Then my poems start
Out of hours Moonlighting sky
Why O why
One's heart can be broken
When yearnings floating
Dancing and shake
Like the force of a quake
As rivers course flowing
For when we touch
The night is a reminder
When passion will flare
Like your smile lights everywhere
And why I miss you so much

WHILE YOU WAIT
BY JOE

How can I believe
About her love
How can I
Feel her eternal love
Trust the one
Forever
I beg to the skies
To be the only one
Enough to hold her
Till our fever flies
A kiss of good night
Caressing her wet hair
Before and after morning
The love on your finger trips
the up and down
A feeling within
The movement of deeps
And bouncing heart beats
The routine according
Hopping she loves me
Like the rose holding
In her lap deepest sleeps.

WE ARE All WARRIORS
BY JOE

Pain is not a funny game
As life a sweet offering
Both in abundance
A surprising twisting flame
Arrows pointed at a ring
Hopefully one's heart distance
In between one's living
There will be dire voyages
Grievances of serious matter
Storms of the universe giving
That will surely encourage us
We try daily forget various worlds
The pain within and of one other
Forgive and all whatever

A DEEPEST KISS
BY JOE

Dropping rain
Yet again
Cooling
What's warming
A love unfolding
Inquisitive flames
Of a touching
Unknown being
A love one claims
The winter rains
And the snowing
Brightening sun rays
Of highly mountains
Going down to sea bays
A kissing foreseen
By the feeling
Of one's skin
The wet of togetherness
Passionately arising
But not surprising
She is my loveless.

A DORMENT TAVIRA
(The Town where I grew up.)
BY JOE

After the heat of summer
And rushes to be calm
Far from all the drama
We meet our inner realm

Like a walk on night's light
Given by the silenced step
Thoughtful pace and bright
Along where's no one yet

Passing one's moment
And night flowers aromas
Alone thoughts persistent
Travelled by the Romans

The Visigoths and Fenicios
Celts and Moors
And romantic lovers suspicious
Drunks and wise indoors.

A FAREWELL KISS
BY JOE

That morning
Of the deepest love
Some powerful few
days upon rivers
Greens of a streaming
Floating pleasures
Searching highly mountains
And springtime roses
Searching for a light
In meadowsweet fields
When you are not there
But you always shining
When I'm dreaming
That thought that sustains
My verses and proses
A lightning that feels
And stars awakening
Yesterday's emotions
But loving you
And the love that is
And the kiss forgotten
When time played
My loving kiss

A GIRL WITH A SMILE
BY JOE

She smiles everyday
Even when candles burn
Adventurers on a run
When kids are at play
She measures the night
Like the moon rotation
Hoping a brighter light
Lifting one's relaxation
Her beautiful everything
A woman that's shining
A lovingly kind of thing
That a man wishing dinning
So the story unfolding
A woman warrior
Yet calmness holding
To be a survivor is her.

A GOOD ADVICE
BY JOE

Life has its troubles
Teach your children
How to play marbles
A ring of roses
Not to hinder
The art of proses
Look at them
As light of the Sun
Like a flower stem
Towards it run
Lift their hands up high
Fill their dear soul
With wisdom of the sky
The love to be loved
A compassionate all
The being of your illusion
Just because learning
An experience conclusion
Let them play
And live their own way.

A LIFE'S SPLENDOUR
BY JOE

I woke upon springtime
By the breaths of living
Beneath smiles of this Earth and
Flowers richer buds
A smiling sunlight
Flowering meadowsweet
Woodlands of love
Freshly and pure
Like a morning sun
Colouring one's mind
Purple pink
Reds and browns
The dark of your skin
A place of destiny
Unknown by words
But by only
Shadows of the sea

A LIGHT OF SPIRIT
BY JOE

Inside of your Soul
Within all
There is always light
Breathing a sigh
Pay attention
Of your dimension
Have energetic thoughts
Not tied bursting knots
Create illuminance
Sing and dance
Let go of yesterday
But enjoy this day
Reach for the skies
And forget the lies
Awake your dormant sleep
Look within and deep
Light up your weight
Transform your state
Feel the inner vibes
That the spirit describes
Born yet again
Without any pain
See a loving paradise
Awaiting in disguise.

A LOVE HIDDEN
BY JOE

I don't see you anymore
But my dreams
Of you like before
Are staying alive
The things we adore
Our talking raves screams
The loving our time
That you would still
Love one lovers dreams
And so we go
Like a treadmill
Waving a goodbye
Around and going slow
A beautiful woman
A secret of a land
Far away from a kissing
That any man's hand
Give her his all living.

A LOVE UNKNOWABLE
BY JOE

Afar in the vastest horizon
There is a girl of my dreams
A wishing thinking
So it seems
Like a flowering garden
She lights mysterious
Fields of a heart giving
A road longer than space
Galaxies far away
A love not notorious
To feel a warm embrace
To be with whatever may
Between the dawn of Sunrise
And the Sun's hidden place
Behind the Earth's cluster
Like a person dreamed in disguise
But the beauty
I feel must be her.

A LOVING WOMAN
BY JOE

Like a star you shine
Across the Cosmos infinite
A woman that could be mine
A whisper I must admit

Her caring softness
A wish of worlds unknown
One's soul restlessness
By strongly winds blown

A gathering of intense waves
Like her hair flowing
A taste of her lips shapes
The place where I'm going

A love not be ever lost
Like the beauty of her eyes
No matter one's cost
I'm going into the skies

The words between said
Of loving day could be
As the universe once had
A blast and that maybe.

A MAGICAL WOMAN
BY JOE

Do not be afraid
By the love that is given
Because she turns darkness
Into light
Her love stands by you
She will come to your aid
And all be forgiven
As tears of past Inverness
going through
Another mountain climbed
Staying together
Of tears and laughter
And the inner sublime
That stars shine forever
With love therein after.

A PATH OF LIGHT
BY JOE

Of all walks of life
And a thousand steps
A soul of darkness fear
Blocked in inner chains
Awaiting falling rains
And a sky to clear
Any doubting depths
That you been and strive
A living throughout
One's space and time
The passage to be yourself
Everything that is in
Have and never doubt
One's unique voyage climb
Or whatever else
Belongs of a streaming within.

A PORTUGUESE AVENTURA
BY JOE

This is SAGRES a reminder
Of other ships
That for centuries
Left ashore
And the farewell arbour
For all relationships
A goodbye to families
Those you adore
A SAUDADE...The longing
Forever apart unknowing
What Oceans
A travelling soul will end
Battered by storms Darkness of the sea
What emotions
Of rain you can stand
Wet to one's bones
Why not you but me
Strong as a pillar
Defying the unknown
Times of wood and stones
Like a magical healer
Throwing it's spell
Where to go and roam
A voyage of Warriors
And to do well.

A SEARCH OF LIGHT
BY JOE

The wishing sunlight
On the horizon bright
Before the coming night
And the waiting standstill
For the love that will
Build that stone and steal
A hut on a river
Where love is a giver
And passion is eager
The fire wood place
Together we embrace
As the flames race
A dancing in blasting fire
A togetherness desire
For a Moonlight to admire

A SLEEPLESS FLOWER
BY JOE

She wishes someone
To love
The love going by
Timing that rushes
Her beating heart
That man of paradise
A hunter
For her loving cry
From a land of broken
Heart adventurers
She still cultivates
Her wishing aromas
Falling from mountains high
A flavour of hope
A sea of deeply romance
Blue mysterious
Mirrored by sunlight
And the unique sky
Warming her lost soul
Brighten her smile
Before the scheduled flight
Of the Moon
Takes away her love
And a morning cry

A SUMMER'S MOONLIGHT
BY JOE

We were young
We met at bar
Thus so far
We were strong
Full of living
And believing
That nothing will be wrong
A date of joyful pleasure
That summer treasure
The laughter
A whisper something
Lips touching
Me and her
A tomorrow's Sun
Fastening run
Feelings of lovers
By the silenced night
Keeping us thigh.

A WARRIOR'S FIGHT
BY JOE

In the land of love
You must feel the hurt
Days of sunshine
Welcoming the bright
Lights from above
Beyond one's dirt
Fighting a peaceful
peace of mind
Loving for nothing
But a moment
Of adoration kind
Strong as the wings
Of a spirit of mine
Bounded universal life
Between this Earth
And a spiritual realm
The ache of one's blood
Not yet understood
By the hurtful wishing
The meaning of calm

A WIND'S BREEZE
BY JOE

One's thoughts of you
Persistent as the night
Alone by whispers
Of the moonlight
Together a breathless
Suspended space
An emotional lost
One's soul restlessness
A beating heart race
Dusting gloom at a cost
Bonds of loving you
As I speak to the winds
Enjoyment of flowers
My heart entering
Your garden of sins
A forbade silence
Traveling like the moon
As a lunatic pathway
With the abundance
Of the sea oceans
To embrace you soon

A WOMAN IS ...
BY JOE

A woman is life
She travelled a mountain
Across all pain
Along rivers
Passing by...
The fields that sustain
A world ..
The mother of time
And living Earth
She gives
One's birth
A light
Everything

A WOMAN'S WISH
BY JOE

Secrets are hidden
In a forest
In a deep sea
Beneath
One's own soul
depths
Yet for coming
Just like shadows
Becoming light
The hurting
Tears
Future hopes
And dreams
A woman with passion
With so much
To give
Freedom last
Till love
Imprisoning
One's heart
A Earth sun
A shining
A winter's moonlight
The unknowing
The skies
The wish
A moment
To be loved
To be cared
To be everything
And a woman.

A WOMAN'S CAUSE
BY JOE

Moonbeams lights her beauty
Beyond anything
Even from mountains
Shadows
But the wind's whispering
I can only taste
Her sweaty
Mountain valleys
And trees dancing
Places far from
My town walking alleys
In which I dwell
I could go freely
A walking step
Or a trip from the soul
That may be well
To be dearly kept.

HOPE YOU WELL
BY JOE

Hope the sky
Is shining bright
This morning day
And pain gone away
And your sleep
Is quietly deep
A dream that softens
That lighting opens
Like a cloudy Moonlight
Begging the shining light
Powered by the Sun
And the enjoyable fun
Coming to please
And take you at ease
The wish of me
And take you free.

AS I WALK
BY JOE

As I walk my steps
Towards life I know
As my own soul depths
Knowing a destiny far ago

As I walk the written story
Of a course of light and pain
I walk for hope and glory
Till the universe stars rain

As I walk for a promise land
Where love is a reality
I pass on the Earth's end
To find out where to be

As I walk for a while
Within all there
And deep I see one's smile
That living is everywhere

BEST NO UNDERWEAR
BY JOE

It starts with one's touch
That feeling
Without rush
A mutual movement
Coordination living
The moment
Passionately arising
The hidden skin
A fever surprising
Both within
Waters of discovery
Melted between sweat
Cry loud of destiny
Drenched and wet
Nowhere to hide
But the flying clothes
By the bed side
A tomorrow's notes.

BY THE MOUNTAINS
BY JOE

Blowing breeze meadowsweet
Down below
Like Springfield's flowers
She loves the wind
And sunny colourways
A blow
And the grass hidden
By the winter snow
A begging of Spring
Mating bird's songs
Bound by valleys
Of love
Unfolding beauty
A breath of freshness
Wondering soul
Facing the horizons
Cascading mists
Of a morning rainbow
And silver lining
Mirroring her
Shining of mountains
Faraway from oceans
Where she wants to go
Tales of rivers quietly crying.

FIRST ENCOUNTER
BY JOE

In the mid - afternoon breeze
We laid our famine bodies on a warm field grass
Our eyes transmitted wild passionate hunger
Yet the serenity of our soft touch
Was like a limpid crystal stream
Docile on its way
We caressed between tall trees and wilderness
We felt fever engulfing like strips of fire
Bombarded sky high by a volcano of love
Our hearts pumped running blood as lava
Meanwhile, taking away your
Glamorous hair - clip
I touch your hair waves
Extending aromas
Giving my palate uncharacteristic thirst
And the gentleness of my lips
Finding your sensuality around your neck
With your eyes closed
And deeper breathing
Your murmurs sounds of lovable drunkenness
In that moment there is no existing time but us
And a butterfly passing by
Smiling at happy vibes
Composing melodies with its wings
Of love
Wishful desire and burning fire

DREAMING DESIRE
BY JOE

I dreamed of you
When the nightlife was quite
Only my turmoil
and your silenced sleep
The slow continuously
Breaths
Of your moving chest
A voice of yesterday
My nightly desire
Like the Moon
Loves the Sun
Warming Earth
When dusk falls
And Stars brighten
The sky
Similar as the shining
Of your darkness hair
Awaiting my gentle stroke
And steadily provoke
Why I certainly awoke.

FOR FRANCE
BY JOE

In a world of ignorance
Betrayed by others
But we know France
Has culture powers
A great Nation
By all liberty
Of human kind notion
But a blind identity
Ruled by evil minds
A living of darkness
Of the worst kinds
Destroying the world
Our living harmony
Descending a cold
Raves of a bad enemy
But the love of spiritual
Is ever stronger
That exists within all

I AM HERE...ALWAYS
BY JOE

Approaching distant sunset,
Together a light,
Crispy dry wind is blowing
Intensively from the north;
Eagerly rushes
Through the clear blue sky.
As it advances
Stronger emphatic gushes
Are destined to her port.
Going south in its direction,
Dancing movements
Of perfection,
Embracing eternity
Of affection;
Until the final blow
Calm and slow,
Soon a rest...A whisper.
And there she is...
Alone...my sweet dear,
Sitting at the end
Of the Old Pier;
Her glorious kind eyes wide open
Yet, misty is the horizon
By the fullness
Of a longing tear.
Her dark brown
Shining long hair,
Floating gentleness
Harmony undulation;
Created...It seems from afar.
She doesn't know
But I'm here.
In sorrow, holding

My Cuban cigar,
The inner crying
Is deeply mutual
And so the inquisitive
Loving sensation.
Yes...I'm right here
But she cannot see me,
Like a systematic routine
A ritual...
Equal as the wind
That constantly blows
Yet, she quiet sits
As her thoughts flows,
Those of intense love
Joy and peace;
The fruits of my direction
The comforter
A present gentleness
That guides her
To smile again
And support her
Her eyes blinked
As the air was getting warmer.
I'm just leaving my promised
Kiss...
Simultaneously tears dropped
Down her face,
Brushed away
By unexpected twirling wind
That came from nowhere
But by the open wide space.
She feels my presence...
And that I still miss.

IF I LIVED IN A FOREST WOODEN SHACK...
BY JOE

In a hard wooden chair
I would sit
Sitting on a decaying table
For centuries balancing
Arms supported of present surreal time
And the continuous flows of silence
A wax candle movements
Burning light dancing
Faithfull at my side
And the incoming breeze
Flowing wind
Moving inquisitive flames
Mysterious shadows
Like a cosmic push
From faraway stars
Where a mind meets
An inner thought
A travelling
Lifting my soul and write
A poem of any kind
Writings that emerge
Same as fire soaring harrows
One's pain of yesterday's
Crying scars
Targeting my lonely
And loving heart
A world of crazy merge
Antagonist by ignorance
Or the absolute equilibrium
And nothing in life
Like the next coming dart
But if I lived in a forest wooden shack
Where's life crystal clear

A wisdom
Versing within my breath
Writing life passages
In semi - darkness
Conversing with the sky
Outside walking along
The Silver river near
And the margins of gold
Yet to be met
My learning spiritual
Ascension

IS SHE LISTENING
BY JOE

What does love sounds
Whispering softness
Into her ears
Prisoners of space
And timeless
Hours of time rounds
Like thrown spears
Against one's heart
As one keeps going on
For days lesser then years
Before the morning birds
Singing their own songs
Of love as a spirit born
Grateful for being loved
Adored by nature's mystery
A force unknown
By opening one's heart
And listening slow
Deepest beats you see.

LA FEMME
BY JOE

After a long day
She relaxes
In a foam bath
For a while
With a glass of wine
Une femme du jour
Mais pas sans vrais amour
Maybe she will stay
For a little longer
Warming her pensamientos
That 'demain" is another day
Et toujour one's trip
That one endure
Coisas da vida tormentos
That come and go
Or wake or asleep
Yet she's love
Stronger that any storm
Coming from one's
Universe and stars
Like an angel from above

LIFE IS A RIVER
BY JOE

Bare feet in Santa Luzia
I've walk muddy paths
I've played youthful games
And river many baths,
Growing up in Tavira
I had dusty old shoes
Good as brown news
Friends lived as equal
Like Sardines swimming
Happily in a shawl of friendship
A blissfully time mutual,
Like the rising morning sun
and the nightly Moon
You can never run
But rivers
Flowing one's life
That living paradise
Love gain and lost
Sandy beaches
Romancing with a cost
The play
The real living
A time of beauty
There is no replay

LIFE'S JOURNEY
BY JOE

This Earth
This Heaven of mine
Of mine illusion mind
My dreaming canvas
Air breeding
Wishing flying
Away...windy dances
Why am I
Wondering
Thinking around reality
The wall of walls
And a clear sky
Betrayed by life
Squash by pain
A loaf of bread
fish of the sea arrive
Survival sustain
A man of bad luck
Mountains climbed
Made of steel
Swamp by songs
Of a violin struck
Close to paradise
A burning feeling
That all sounds well

LIFE'S SHADOW
BY JOE

I have felt
The Earth's pain
Pulsing
Beats
And heavy breath
Who am I
That feels
One's mystical
Cry
Born of darkness
And lighting
Nightmarish dreams
Dreadful wilderness
Trapped
A warrior's cross
Mercy and strength
By God's wrath
Dancing love
Shadows
A rhythm of time
Like flying arrows
Crushing
Into the night

MY LITTLE HOUSE
BY JOE

When the dawn is coming
A calming warming
brightening
The solitude
Of a night
A dream misunderstood
An awakening
Up there right
A little bit
Where lovers grow
And fire lit
A burning desire
Kissing a morning go
Giving it all
The wishing sunlight
Whatever
Big and small
But my little home
Will be forever

ONE'S ENDLESS SEARCH
BY JOE

Consider the millennium
Our descendants
The creators of gods
Destroyers of peace
Humanity of a common place
Believers of a destination
Religious clubs
Meaningless fights
So much inner pain
A father of the skies
Where happiness lies
Centuries of ignorance
As the prosperous rain
Becomes waterfalls nuisance
A paradise lost
By greed and anger
Thousands of sensations
All human creations
Human kind imaginations
A world outside expectations
Seeking divine
Everlasting pleasure

PASSION IS FIRE
BY JOE

In the valleys of desire
Mountains were climbed
The Picos of fire
Volcanic eruptions
Higher emotions
Sky high ascending
Cosmos stars burning
Till ever time is over
An infinite voyage
Of discovery
A searchable pleasure
Like an hidden treasure
A lost identity
Part of your baggage
Things that you know
Like salt crystals
Creators of miracles
And disappearing snow

SHE IS MY HEART
BY JOE

I'm not talking about
Her beautiful lips
Or her black hair
But the caressing
Falling asleep
On my caring chest
An embrace
Of touching
A togetherness
But the loving moments
Of one's existence
Feeling her heart beat
That love is near
Like a blooming flower
Of the deepest roots
A place that you sit
Faraway torments
But a beating
Of pulsing power

SPIRITUAL LOVERS
BY JOE

Before we were on this
Earth
We met before
Where there was no
Hurt
The loving arena of warrior's
Greatest love
The divine space
A birth
One's Kingdom
The forever coexisting
Like a fearless
Fire burn
Souls of the stars
Of yesterday closeness
Heart run
The pulsating beat
Of a desired light
Hidden
Between a woman
And a man

SWORDS WITHOUT WORDS
BY JOE

The first strike
Towards one's flesh
Near your heart
The silenced night
Keeping your own rest
Believing that the company
Is your worldliness
Betrayed by tongues
Ever speechless
Right and wrongs
A flying coming dart
Yet again aimlessly
Far from one's own pain
Nowhere near as the start
The love lost by you and me
And arrows come

TENDERNESS KISS
BY JOE

How I can wait for the day
To set your heart free
And kiss you so tenderly
A longing every day
And the way
I love your smile
Your kind words
Floating around
If only for a while
Whispers of time
A wish in the dark
Awaiting for light
Quietly abandoned
And here to listen
That Heaven's spark
Between higher mountains
You must fly
Even against swerving winds
Stronger then I
Or chariots of gold
Galloping that high
But a love that brings
Fables of love to be hold.

THAT EMOTIONAL
BY JOE

She dreamed of a rainbow
Full of hopping colouring
A wishing portrait
Painted years ago
She hold on at clouds moving
And at a sunny light up straight

She cried of deeply emotions
When night was at its highest
Tears descending
Cascades of oceans
And love lost mightiest
Gone forever ending

She woke up tumbling
Morning stars arising
A breeze of time
Clarity of light assembling
That moment and timing
When living is mine.

THAT SUMMER
BY JOE

When I saw your smiling
Adorable looks
Eyes of light
Hiding shy
Pinkish lips
With a smile
Facial naughtiness
Awaiting the unknown
The magical spark
An opportunity
Of love
Pleasing the Sun
The heated moment
And flowers breeze
A flowing cooling wind
Waking one's destiny
Me and you
Created a storming
Harmony
Bodies of rhythm
Without poetry
Rhymes of times
Of a tomorrow's poem
The unforgettable love
True to afternoons fields
And the cry of Moonlight

THE ANGEL
BY JOE

I had a dream tonight
Causing me a shivering fright
The light
Upon my losing soul
A tumbling moment
Like I was tired of this Earth
But in Heaven's power
With gracious silenced delight
I arose from my dying bed
Looking at this lovely being
Dressed in feathers long and White
Teaching me that all races
The love within us all
Has no colour
That one's learning
Are life
So in an shapeless
Logical existing form
A sweet arm close to me
At my sight
And in a hurry
The celestial love
Rushed to help
Others and fill their
Heart.

THE AWAKENED
BY JOE

You are what you are
What others can't be
A book written
On one's flesh
A story unfolding
And miles of scribbling
Words never complete
Only the insisting
Of a deeper insight
With comprehension
A life of luminosity
Another dimension
Free of society
The awakening mind
People of a different kind
Born to be everyone
And to live as one.

THE FLAME
BY JOE

One's soul is burning
stoves of living
Fires upon rivers
Margins running
Ever giving
But one's solitude shivers
The ignorance
At your feet
For instance
An immense heat
Boiling water fields
Overcoming shaded
Gardens of peaceful flow
The timing heals
They say...rated
You stay or you go
The night is upon
One's impertinence
A nonsense
Why you not gone

THE FLOW OF WATERS
BY JOE

As the rain falls
Down to Earth
So the Sun rays
There after
Warming a space
A coldness of souls
Becoming dirt
Tears of passing days
Floating matter
An oceanic race
Kissed by dried mountains
Loved by rocky streams
Embraced by growing rivers
All that is and sustains
Daylight hours dreams
Waters of life givers
Cascades down coming
An experience
The unavoidable path
Towards you running
A reality existence
Of a cold and warm bath.

THE SPIRITUAL KIND
BY JOE

Hundred years of fighting
Beforehand the plains lakes and riverside flames
The tribesmen claims
Our land spiritual protected
As the wolf and the sky Eagle's flight
Free without sleepless chains
A horse riding and I am
Courage without fear
Carved by all it remains
A warrior of peace and light
The race against the moving white men
By nature's depths betrayed
Yet by ignorance propelled
Same as today's world
A river of blindness
Of highly mountains
Flowing regardless
If it rains or snow
But nature surviving
Into to the arms of the unknown.

THE WARRIOR OF PEACE
BY JOE

Of all burdensome life
And storms and darkness
Of existing pain
Be patient
Because all will arrive
Be considered in harnesses
Feel your own strain
Knock open your heart
And shine the doors
Of yesterday's crying
By the morning sun start
The one that will adores
And fight for you dying
A warrior's strength
From a unknowing world
With the light of above
And wings far length
Larger than a heart cold
But a fighter for Love.

THE WINDS OF A WOMAN
BY JOE

She dreamed all alone
Asleep every time
Broken by day
Broken by night
Tears like rain
Falling upon a stone
Teardrops
Those unique feelings
Like Earth deceivingly
Giving an apple and a snake
Missing born innocent
And the curtain drops
She abandons living
Yet she is the creation
Of anytime
Like the blowing wind
That caresses her hair
She gives life.

THE WISHING WILD
BY JOE

Look around you
What are you looking
Are your thoughts free
Or a stone deathly
Bashed by a century
Of a soul living price
The hopefully none sin
The wishing life
Little things to begin
That love will arise
As a winning star
Shining nearest
Close to feathers fields
And the one dearest
Being what you are.

THERE AGAIN A WOMAN
BY JOE

From a voyage
A distance
Telling my own secrets
To a world
Out of my mind
A promise listen
Like a first time
A purest love
To last it's very root
Faithfull and kind
words of man
As time goes by
A universe intent
Songs of promise rain
Of a touching soft
Moonlight
And ponds
Deep as a sea
Shifting light
Illuminating
Yesterday's stories
And dreams
Like you can see
By you
And travelling
By me.

THERE ALWAYS A FIRE
BY JOE

Voices were heading
Calls rushed
away
Friends togetherness
A warmth
Faraway
Places displaced
And night
Brightness Moon
Gathering light
And dancing
Pretty soon
Forgetting not
The intended fire
Conversational mode
Of life
And the universe
Times present
Memories

THERE AN ANGEL
BY JOE

In the inner universe
A transient warm breeze
A wave of brightness
Peace and homelike rest
Sitting and writing ease
Luminosity beyond darkness

The finest inner lining
Directions of living
Abandoned by lying
Ravaged by a breath of air
Yesterday's dreaming
Times gasped by despair

The love to be loved
Way and way faraway
A sweetness by gone stoned
Aromatique winds sway
A garden freshness lost
But her beauty has a cost

As the passing breeze flows
Tears are dropped slowly
A remembrance of sorrows
An emotional heart sinking
Bled by harrows throws

But a return of life passion
Her smile again
Serene upon my flame
And her satisfaction
There was no one to blame
But wings flying in the rain.

THIS IS YOUR LIFE
BY JOE

Born in world
Full of pleasure
Things of wonder
Breaths of living
Stars that glimmer
Gravity to hold
A capacity closure
Comforting thunder
Thoughts and dreams
Understanding spiritual
Eternity souls
Life's greatest mysteries
One's internal nature
Where the spirit goes
A flight never known
But wishing the heavens
Thinking that never flows
Until the end of time
The passage to be
To be at peace
Of a touching world
real and close presence
Of being between these.

THIS JOURNEY IS OUR JOURNEY
BY JOE

In life one loses a few dreams
A dance in the rain
A sunset of a lovable day
The walk on touching hands
A time invisible
But sounds of a river
Streams
A beach romancing sands
Darker skies to clime
A lonely journey
The impossible
But a quieter wind
Moving heavy clouds
From lands afar
Then a blissful morning
Rays of pleasure
Suffered by waves of sea
And a direction of light
A mysterious traveller
Of a mid-sky dreaming
Descended
With a smile and laughter

THIS WORLD OF OURS
BY JOE

Darkened by darkness
Souls of this living
Life of madness
Existing for killing
Destruction of peacekeeping
Distorted mindfulness
This time of our existence
No change prehistoric
The same rhetoric
This humans does my head in
Ok... I can think so do you
Why we are this kind to sin
To betray and savage
Like unreasonable animals
Tell me about your voyage
About love and hate
What's on your mind intervals
Deep hidden thoughts of late
Do you lay down or have courage
To change an impossible world
Our beautiful love for each other
This planet dying spinning bowl
Waiting for your changes brother.

THOUGHTS BY THE RIVER
BY JOE

A breeze holding
Love
A river crying
Ripping open
Tears and memories
A brain spin
To the past
Profoundly sweet
Mountains above
A sheltered hope
From wind and rain
And that emotional pain
Yet a mind stillness
Like a rainbow
Teaching a flower
How to grow
Blooms of the skies
Sun rays
The unveiling wand
Of gardens colouring
A wish upon
Of a night
A missing light
Shades of passion
Flows of a river
Like her thoughts
On and on.

TO BE LOVED BY THEE
BY JOE

I await
To be loved
And love with passion
Like Springfield's flowers
Caressing the winds
One's reaction
What Summer brings
A reaching soul
For your beauty
Hopes and a gloomy
Of deeply Oceans
Like a heart
Must carry on
Behind timeless pains
Smiles with a mask
A missing part
Breathing emotions
Like a whisper in time
Wishing sun but rains
To live at your side
The need of life
That may go
Same as a dancing night
And the softness
Of a Moonlight.

TO LIVE WITHOUT LOVE
BY JOE

It hurts one's soul
Living without love
Like a voice crying
Thrown and shattered
Where only darkness
Is screaming
For light
The void of loneliness
Echoing walls of pride
Consumed by failures
And missing
The joys of life
Emptiness
Without comfort
Doubts unsustainable
Showered by tears
Weaknesses
Of a time
An out of reach
Hope
A struggle
Of pain
Like everyone else
But when it rains
All seems pointless
You come back
Bouncing
And dancing
With fire
On your veins .

TO YOU MY PRINCESS
BY JOE

In my dream world
I see you clearly
As I fight to sleep
But I'm often told
That I love you dearly
Down there and deep

I see your struggles
Of life and darkest skies
A path missed flowers
all my heartfelt cuddles
Like my dormant eyes
Lost of extremes powers

I see you walking
In a vast wilderness
Where the clouds are dark
For love you looking
Somehow in distress
Awaiting that coming spark

As I turn to my right
And yet again to my left
I found myself on my back
Like I was having a fight
Something that I felt
In loving you in the dark.

TWO SOULS BURNING
BY JOE

When love is a flame
Burning inside
In the hearts of beings
A moment in time wave
A life's greatest ride
The strongest of feelings
An emotion not seen
But felt in one's soul
Like the sky at night
A sparkling universe screen
Of stars on a flying roll
Wide as a loving heart
A magnetic connection
By fieldworkers near
Pulled by Earth's energy
Winds throwing direction
To a warm-hearted dear
Love her with intensity.

WAVES OF SORROW
BY JOE

Your Longing love danced
On the crest of foam
Moving to sands
Near the shore of my soul
The battling ship
Against higher rocks
And your crying salty tears
Hopelessly
Hanging in distress
To the mast your embrace
Missing hugs
Never voyage
Lost in shadows
Your eyes surrender
Cracking sounding waves
Splitting the boat in two
Forever
Into the deep abyssal
Oceans was our love
Troubled as the momentum
Sea storm
Bombastic romance
Travelling far
To nowhere
Resounding Echoing
Of your voice
So near
Kissing nothing
But the winds
Presence...

WE WERE FRIENDS
BY JOE

How time passes
A flashing
Like a blinking
In one's eyes
Flown
At this morning dawn
By winds
Of yesterday
closeness between
Our friendly love
But time...
Time lossless
And therein
All forgotten
Like the smiles
We shared
Playing for miles
Of living
As we always dared
A innocence
Not believing
What the future brings
That friends will go
Maybe forever
Some stay in sunny springs
Like flowers blossoming
For a season
Others never
Only awaiting
For your giving hand
And forgiveness
As shinning morning.

YESTERDAY
BY JOE

Sometimes we say
Words out one's way
Said by a talking day
A moment of disarray
Winds that sway
On the loving sea bay
Lying on waves faraway
But for the love we stay
And always pray
That a shining ray
A wishing togetherness may
Clear the skies grey...away.

YOUR TEARS
BY JOE

Why do you cry
Tell me why
You ranted
I stayed
I was afraid
And donned
Why this tears
Dropping
Like spears
Harrows the wind
Never stopping
Flying to one's heart
Dreamlike pain
A reality start
An infinite voyage
No one's domain
But sorrows
A togetherness baggage
Lost in an airport
A goodbye tomorrows
We will never support
A love forgotten ...
And that's why
We do cry.

Biography

My Portuguese name is José but I'm known as Joe.

I was born in the picturesque town of Tavira in the Algarve, southern Portugal. My parents ancestors and family came from a fishing village 1.5 miles west called Santa Luzia, where I lived till I was 12 years old. This beautiful fishing village became known in Portugal as the 'Capital of the Octupus'.

When I was 13 years old I got a job in a Café/Snack Bar in Tavira public garden near the River Gilão during the school summer holidays. There I learned the trade and became a waiter at 17. I worked there till I was 27.

The first time I visited the UK was in 1985 to see friends, and I continued doing so every year till I moved permanently in 1989. I initially worked in a restaurant in Crystal Palace, London.

In 1990 I went travelling to South East Asia and Australia. In Phuket Island, Thailand I got bitten by an infected mosquito and got Dengue fever feeling badly ill. As we know people die from it. Happily, I recovered.

I got married in 1991 to a Reverend's daughter in Suffolk, UK. And from this marriage I have 2 beautiful daughters, Eleanor and Madalena.

I took a Diploma of Higher Education from Warwick University in European studies, comprising European History and Culture, Sociology, Philosophy and French.

After the breakup of my marriage I moved from Gloucestershire to West Sussex, where I still live today.

My career has included a job at Gatwick airport working in the detention centre for illegal immigrants. From there I moved on to work in the caring environment working with people suffering from conditions such as cerebral palsy, autism, alcohol and drug abuse, MS and providing end of life care. Today I work as a Health Care Assistant working with elderly people.

Printed in Great Britain
by Amazon